PRIMITIVE
CHRISTIANITY

BY GRANT EDWARDS

PRIMITIVE CHRISTIANITY

Published by:

Visionary Dreamers (Pty) Ltd

Registration Number: 2014/099200/07

1256 Plakkie Street, Toekomsrus 1759, Johannesburg,

Gauteng Province, RSA

Website: www.elroyrcook.com

E-Mail: info@elroyrcook.com

Printed in South Africa

ISBN

Paperback: 978-0-620-80415-8

EBook: 978-0-620-80416-5

CONTENTS

ENDORSEMENTS

Apostle Grant Edwards' Primitive Christianity is definitely a must read for all those desiring a deep meaningful walk with God. It speaks to all who seek to understand the "How to's" of God.

Having been discipled and mentored by Apostle Grant Edwards, we know that all his teachings focused on practical demonstration by the Holy Spirit in line with Holy Scripture.

Primitive Christianity is born out of Apostles Grant's walk and ministry with God.

It will challenge the reader to truly evaluate their relationship with God. Though titled "primitive", it is everything but that, written in conjunction with the Holy Spirit it offers deep revelation, wisdom, and insight.

Roger and Lesley-Ann De Wet
Co-founders
Benjamin Mentorship Project SA

After reading Primitive Christianity, I came to the understanding that Christianity is an inward journey. It also allowed me to have a clear picture that Christ in me is my foundation. It has helped me to flow in gifts of the Holy Spirit and thus making my walk with God an exciting journey. The manner in which the book was written is very practical making it easy to understand. I highly recommend it, especially if you believe in the supernatural power of God.

Robin Weber

The book Primitive Christianity has changed my life not only because of the book itself but because of the person who writes the book, when reading it you see yourself already doing what is being taught.

It's like you see yourself already doing what the scripture says because of how the Holy Spirit speaks to you while reading the book.

Victor Lottering

Primitive Christianity is must read masterpiece for any Christian earnestly aspiring to build a solid personal relationship with the Lord God or the trinity. It provokes the anointing in a Christian believer, by challenging one through foundational truth of our faith. Pointing out in a believer the effectual and reality of God's Word! As well as helping a Christian believer to look within oneself and discover the

Christ. Our true foundation on which any Christian is to build and grow their hope, faith and love, in "Christ the very blueprint and master builder of our lives". It also makes aware God's will to reveal himself to any believer. The book helps one to be emboldened through the language of the Holy Spirit. While placing any believer on the very pedestal of the heroes of faith, clarifying to a Christian believer the state of engagement with the trinity and the heavenly realms.

Musonda Molewa
I AM Ministries

Grant Edwards shares spiritual truths in his book, 'Primitive Christianity', in a simple and easy way. I enjoyed the book and found the insights easily digestible. As a reader who was also personally observed the writers ministry, I can see he communicates these truths here, in the same way that others experienced the power of God in his ministry — clear, raw and unmistakable. This is a very enjoyable read indeed.

Ryan Jacobs
Ministry Leader - The Enpowered Church

FOREWORD

My first encounter with my father in the faith came way back in 2000 in a home cell meeting to which I was invited. Here was a man of God whom later as I would discover would teach me the deeper truths of the Spirit of God and the Word of God. When I first met him, I saw how God would use him in such a simple yet profound manner in not only teaching the Word of God but also then afterwards allowing the Lord to work with him to confirm this very Word with signs following (Mark 16:20).

I was in awe and astounded that God was being revealed and demonstrated in such a practical, yet simple way, and then I asked myself, "How can this be that you can just allow the Word to be taught and then that very same moment, God shows up and confirms the Word you teach with signs following?"

I would later discover that out of close fellowship with the Spirit of God and meditation in the Word of God, this was available to all believers, which the Spirit of the Lord would later on teach me and show me through my father in the faith.

I had so many questions in this meeting and even afterwards that baffled my mind, "How could this be and how was it even possible and is this only for an elite few or is this available for myself as well?" I would then see my Dad in meetings go up and move in the Gifts (Manifestations) of the Spirit with such a tangible sense of the presence, and the power of the Lord would move not only into the meetings but also upon all the people present as the Lord would then speak through His Anointed Servant, Apostle Grant Edwards. This created in me a hunger to meet with him personally and to discover and know the how to's of the Word of God. I wanted to see what he saw and to know what he knew and to have what he had. This desire and hunger would move me to a path and journey of cultivating a hunger and the same relationship with the Spirit of God as he had.

I wish I could say this happened immediately but truth be told, my journey of the *how to* would only start close to 9 months later, but oh boy, it was truly worth the wait. Why that long? This was the same question I asked Dad and he said that the Spirit of the Lord instructed him to "teach faithful men who are able to teach others also," and this is what he wanted to confirm was in me. All along this journey of waiting, I kept on asking him whether the Lord said anything to him about the time being now and he would advise not yet but when the time was ripe, my life was, is and forever will be changed because of that.

I am a living witness to the book that you, dear reader, hold in your hand today. This is no ordinary book and neither is this something that will just supply and provide you with more information. What you hold in your hand today is Revelation with Manifestation that will bring *Impartation* into your own personal walk and relationship with the Lord. Get ready to embark upon a journey of discovering, practically with proven results and countless testimonies, the how to's of God when it comes to the miraculous.

What you will receive from this book "Primitive Christianity" is the Ability to become a modern-day Miracle Worker, a modern-day Living Epistle—one who will demonstrate that Jesus Christ is indeed the same Yesterday, Today and Forever. You will no longer see yourself as one whom God cannot use for the move of the Spirit of God, neither will you minister and see nothing happen. By the end of this book, you will discover that God is a practical God and that He can use even you, the ordinary saint, to do great exploits for His Kingdom!

Surely, you will become the very evidence of God's reality in your life after reading this book. You are a living epistle read of all men, you are an open book that men and women all over the world will read and you are heaven's gift to your generation to reveal and manifest the glory of the Lord!

Child of God, Christian, Son and Daughter of the Living God, get ready to allow God to become so practical in your life where you will know that He is not far but so very near, in your heart and upon your mouth to do wonders! (Romans 8:6-8; 2 Corinthians 4:7-10)

Be blessed as you read.

Yours in Christ,

Jermaine Small

DEDICATION

To my wife Josephine who is in agreement with the call and grace of our Heavenly Father on my life, thank you. You fit the description of what our Heavenly Father spoke through the prophet Amos in chapter 3 verse 3, "Can two walk together, except they be agreed?"

And to my three beautiful daughters, Sabrina Leigh, Barbera Lynne and Joshlynne Kayla, and my little grandson Jordan — my prayer for you is like what Paul mentioned to Timothy, I am praying and asking our Father in heaven, that He make it known to all of you, that not only spiritual sons and daughters can inherit my faith and boldness, but that you, my natural children, will inherit that faith and boldness; as noted in 2 Timothy 1:5, *"When I call to remembrance the unfeigned faith that is in thee, which dwelt first in thy grandmother Lois, and thy mother Eunice; and I am persuaded that in thee also. I am persuaded that my faith and boldness is inherited by all of you."*

And to all the disciples in the School of the Spirit, do not fear the traditions of men that set the word of GOD to naught, but be bold and work miracles, because miracles are proof of GOD's love for the lost.

And last but not least, to my brother born from the same mother and father, Clint Edwards who helped me to get this book out, you are really anointed and gifted in ministry to other nations, hold fast to that grace on your life, thanks a million.

THE PROPER FOUNDATION

Most Christians, who think they are far from God, or God is far from them, think like this because they have never understood that the foundation they received initially was not laid by men, but by God Himself. And in time, men tried to lift up that foundation by laying another, but this time a foundation of their church doctrine and etiquette. I need to say this, that Christianity is not an outward journey, but an inward journey. Look at what the Apostle Paul Said in 1 Corinthians 3:11-13, *"For other foundation can no man lay than that is laid, which is Jesus Christ. Now if any man build upon this foundation gold, silver, precious stones, wood, hay, stubble; Every man's work shall be made manifest: for the day shall declare it, because it shall be revealed by fire; and the fire shall try every man's work of what sort it is."*

Many Christians have a proper foundation, but they allowed men to build on it with wood, hay, and stubble, so when the fire came, it burnt—such believers may still stand today, they are in doubt about their salvation. Then there are those with the wrong foundation, but the right building materials, silver, gold, and precious stones were used to build on the wrong foundation. When the fire tests them, it cannot burn the materials, but because of the foundation, these people do not stand afterward—they sunk because they didn't stand on the proper foundation.

Now Paul said there is no other foundation but that which is ALREADY LAID, WHICH IS JESUS CHRIST. When was it laid? The whole of 1 Corinthians chapter 1 to chapter 3 speaks of teachings that defile the bodies of people and displaces the foundation already laid, which is Christ, by trying to lay another foundation that promotes carnality and contentions amongst believers. 1 John 5:11-12 says, *"And this is the record, that God hath given to us eternal life, and this life is in his Son. He that hath the Son hath life; and he that hath not the Son of God hath not life."* This is speaking about the born-again experience; the day Christ is confessed as Lord and Saviour, He comes into your heart, and with Him comes eternal life from which He cannot be separated. And so, it is necessary for the Christian to journey *inward* to get to know Him—the Christ in you.

Paul says in Galatians 1:15-16, *"But when it pleased God, who separated me from my mother's womb, and called me by his grace, To reveal his Son in me, that I might preach him among the heathen; immediately I conferred not with flesh and blood.*" Paul says, the first thing he had to do was to let God reveal HIS SON IN HIM TO HIM, and once he got to know the SON, which is another name for CHRIST, ANOINTING, UNCTION, DAYSTAR, IMAGE OF GOD, only then he could preach the SON that HE KNEW to the heathen. He could not preach the Christ that PETER, JOHN, or JAMES preached, because there could be no power or witness in that.

Look at what happened in the Bible to those who preach the Christ that someone else preached or operated under, as recorded in Acts 19:13-15, "*Then certain of the vagabond Jews, exorcists, took upon them to call over them which had evil spirits the name of the Lord Jesus, saying, We adjure you by Jesus whom Paul preacheth. And there were seven sons of one Sceva, a Jew, and chief of the priests, which did so. And the evil spirit answered and said, Jesus I know, and Paul I know; but who are ye?*"

Now, this is what happens, when demons or sickness or disease hear you say, "come out in the name of Jesus whom my pastor preaches," even though you mention *Jesus*, they won't give heed to what you say in the natural voice. On hearing that from you, immediately, they know that you have no authority over them, and you cannot drive them out, and things may turn out bad for you.

Matthew 16:13-18 states, *"When Jesus came into the coasts of Caesarea Philippi, he asked his disciples, saying, Whom do men say that I the Son of man am? And they said, Some say that thou art John the Baptist: some, Elias; and others, Jeremias, or one of the prophets. He saith unto them, But whom say ye that I am? And Simon Peter answered and said, Thou art the Christ, the Son of the living God. 17 And Jesus answered and said unto him, Blessed art thou, Simon Bar–jona: for flesh and blood hath not revealed it unto thee, but my Father which is in heaven. And I say also unto thee, That thou art Peter, and upon this rock I will build my church; and the gates of hell shall not prevail against it."*

When Peter said to Jesus, "you are the CHRIST THE SON," Jesus replied "flesh and blood has not revealed this to you," that is, the revelation did not come from man but the Heavenly Father—the Spirit. And the term THIS ROCK refers to the revelation of CHRIST being THE SON OF GOD, of which He said, "I WILL BUILD MY CHURCH, and the GATES OF HELL SHALL NOT PREVAIL against it." In other words, Jesus Christ Himself is the *Foundation*, not Peter as some church denominations claim.

The reason the gates of hell prevail against certain Christians, concerns their foundation. Is Christ or church doctrine their foundation? Romans 8:9 says, *"But ye are not in the flesh, but in the Spirit, if so be that the Spirit of God dwell in you. Now if any man have not the Spirit of Christ, he is none of his."* If the Spirit of Christ is not IN you, then you do not BELONG to him; and then you cannot do the works He did.

Make sure that the mystery that was hidden from ages and generations is not still hidden. Let Christ be revealed to you today. Colossians 1: 26-27 says, *"Even the mystery which hath been hid from ages and from generations, but now is made manifest to his saints: To whom God would make known what is the riches of the glory of this mystery among the Gentiles; which is Christ in you, the hope of glory."* Make sure you know Christ in you and not Christ in another, though He is the same Christ in all. Having a personal relationship— born out of a personal revelation of God to you—is your foundation for walking in the miraculous. Settle that first.

HOW DO I
READ THE BIBLE
AND HEAR THE VOICE OF GOD?

Let me start by saying, the Bible is no ordinary book, and you can most definitely not read it as an ordinary book, because the Bible is the only tangible proof of Heaven in the natural. While reading, you must be in the same place where the words of the Bible were spoken to those who heard it and wrote it because the actions of God and HEAVEN were also seen in this place. If we can get into this place, then what was written can once again come to life.

JESUS Himself said in John 6:63, *"It is the spirit that quickeneth; the flesh profiteth nothing: the words that I speak unto you, they are spirit, and they are life."* The word of God is a living spirit word, and the Apostle Paul said in 2 Corinthians 3:4-6, *"And such trust have we through Christ to God-ward: Not that we are sufficient of ourselves to think anything as of ourselves; but our sufficiency is of God; Who also hath made us able ministers of the new testament; not of the letter, but of the spirit: for the letter killeth, but the spirit giveth life.*" Here, the word of GOD declares that to read and understand his word you have to be dependent on the Spirit to give life to what you read or to what you speak. The key is, the Spirit gives life because the Spirit is the one who spoke the Word in the first place.

2 Peter 1:20-21 confirms this truth, "*Knowing this first, that no prophecy of the scripture is of any private interpretation. For the prophecy came not in old time by the will of man: but holy men of God spake as they were moved by the Holy Ghost.*" So even here in this scripture, it is written that the word of God cannot be privately interpreted, because the word of God did not come by the will man (man did not think it up). Today, there are many Christians who still read the Bible as just another religious book, as they have never trusted God to speak to them for themselves. Even some pastors who preach their sermons on Sundays bring a stale manner or second-hand revelation to the people. They preach someone else's sermon they heard on TV or read in a book.

So where is the place we have to be for the Word to become Spirit and life? And what do we do to be in this place? Revelation 1:10 states, "*I was in the Spirit on the Lord's Day, and heard behind me a great voice, as of a trumpet...*" Where was John? IN THE SPIRIT. What did he hear while being in the Spirit? He heard A VOICE BEHIND HIM. It says in verses 12-13, "*And I turned to see the voice that spake with me. And being turned, I saw seven golden candlesticks; And in the midst of the seven candlesticks one like unto the Son of man, clothed with a garment down to the foot, and girt about the paps with a golden girdle.*"

John not only HEARD with his spiritual ears, but also the EYES of his HEART—imagination—were open to see. And this is the place we must be, that is "IN THE SPIRIT," to read and understand the word of God. That is where God's spoken VOICE is heard, and here is where God acted and the prophets saw that action and heard that voice—and then they wrote it for us to read. This is why the Bible is the only tangible substance from Heaven we have in our hands.

Now to read and understand the Bible, you must know how the voice of the Spirit comes to us in that place called "IN THE SPIRIT." First , the word of God says in Proverbs 20:27 that "*the spirit of man is the candle of the Lord, searching all the inward parts of the belly.*" Your spirit is the dwelling of God, and in this place, He speaks to your spirit—your conscience—by using the voice of your conscience, which sounds like your own voice. As an example, have you ever laid on your bed, and suddenly, you just had a conversation with yourself? It was like debating certain issues in your life, and you argued with yourself in your heart and mind over the issue, but you thought it was just you arguing with yourself. No, no, no, it was not you, it was the Spirit or Christ in you, speaking to you, in that voice of your conscience, giving you advice or wisdom on how to overcome the problem. Your arguing against *that* voice is the voice of reason causing you to doubt the voice of God. That is the voice of GOD which comes to you spontaneously, while the voice of REASON causes you to doubt the wisdom of God being given for your situation.

Always remember Satan (or the voice of reason) never speaks first. His voice of reason always speaks last because he wants you to doubt what God said to you. Genesis 2:16-17 says, *"And the Lord God commanded the man, saying, Of every tree of the garden thou mayest freely eat: But of the tree of the knowledge of good and evil, thou shalt not eat of it: for in the day that thou eatest thereof thou shalt surely die."* GOD SPOKE FIRST here. On the other hand, Genesis 3:1 says, *"Now the serpent was more subtle than any beast of the field which the Lord God had made. And he said unto the woman, Yea, hath God said, Ye shall not eat of every tree of the garden?"* Satan spoke last with the voice of reason which caused doubt and unbelief.

I want to show you the simplicity of Christ.

Matthew 3:16-17 — *"And Jesus, when he was baptized, went up straightway out of the water: and, lo, the heavens were opened unto him, and he saw the Spirit of God descending like a dove, and lighting upon him: And lo a voice from heaven, saying, This is my beloved Son, in whom I am well pleased."* The voice of God spoke first.

Matthew 4: 3 — *"And when the tempter came to him, he said, If thou be the Son of God, command that these stones be made bread."* Satan spoke last and tried to make Him reason and doubt his sonship.

So always, the spontaneous thoughts or voice of God comes to you first, and then the voice of reason which causes you to doubt the first voice. I would suggest you always take a pen and paper while reading the word of God on any subject and write out the first spontaneous thoughts that come to you in the voice of your conscience, and then you'll notice the voice of reason that will cause you to doubt and argue against what you heard. This is how you read the word of God in the Spirit and by the Spirit.

Romans 9:1 says, *"I say the truth in Christ, I lie not, my conscience also bearing me witness in the Holy Ghost."* His conscience bears him witness in the Holy Ghost (the Holy Ghost in his conscience was using the voice of his conscience to speak to him). The best way to exercise this is to always journal what you hear, so you can afterward mark out all the words of reason, against the words of God which is spontaneous and always EDIFIES, COMFORTS and EXHORTS you.

HOW TO
MINISTER THE SPIRIT, PRAY AND RECEIVE IMMEDIATE ANSWERS

First, I want to point to an example in the Scripture on how God gave man exactly what he needed, the moment there was a need. Genesis 2:18 says, *"And the Lord God said, it is not good that the man should be alone; I will make him an help meet for him."* God saw the need in man, and God wanted to supply his need, but He also wanted to teach man how He can supply man with all his needs. And remember that everything God created was outside of man, and God was finished with creating things; so He was in rest, and would not create anything anymore if ever there would be a need again.

We see proof in verse 20 where *"Adam gave names to all cattle, and to the fowl of the air, and to every beast of the field; but for Adam there was not found an help meet for him."* God brought all His creations before Adam and literally said to him, 'Now Adam, I am in rest, all that you name is all that I have created on the outside of you. If ever you have a need, I will create nothing anymore because I am finished working, and you will not find the provision you need on the outside of you, but whatever you'll need will be found on the inside of you. So, all you've got to do is believe it, and name it."

It is written in verse 21, *"And the Lord God caused a deep sleep to fall upon Adam, and he slept: and he took one of his ribs, and closed up the flesh instead thereof."* This is why when we see the Spirit come UP and ON people, we must not disturb them, because God is taking the PROVISION out from inside of them and bringing it to them so they can name it. Now come down to verse 23, *"Adam said, This is now bone of my bones, and flesh of my flesh: she shall be called Woman, because she was taken out of Man."* He named her because "SHE WAS TAKEN OUT OF MAN." Let me show you how God answers our prayer. It is unnecessary to show you how to pray, because all Christians already know how to pray. The problem in Christianity is not in praying but in knowing how to receive the answers or provision asked for.

First, we must understand that the born-again believer has everything he will ever need to put himself over in his lifetime. The Christian is already a winner or victor, with access to all the *fullness* of God. Look at Philemon 1:6, *"That the communication of thy faith may become effectual by the acknowledging of every good thing which is in you in Christ Jesus."* Where is every good thing? Is it not already IN YOU, IN CHRIST? Ephesians 1:3 affirms, *"Blessed be the God and Father of our Lord Jesus Christ, who hath blessed us with all spiritual blessings in heavenly places in Christ."* Where has He already blessed you with EVERY SPIRITUAL BLESSING? Is it not in the HEAVENLY PLACES, IN CHRIST? Let us confirm it again in 2 Peter 1:3, *"According as his divine power hath given unto us all things that pertain unto life and godliness..."* HE HATH (past tense), by His divine POWER, already given us all things. So where is it? Is it not already *in* you? But how is it obtained by us?

Let's go to the word of God again. Luke 1:34-35 states, *"Then said Mary unto the angel, How shall this be, seeing I know not a man? And the angel answered and said unto her, The Holy Ghost shall come upon thee, and the power of the Highest shall overshadow thee: therefore also that holy thing which shall be born of thee shall be called the Son of God."* The question on every man's heart is, how shall this happen? How will God do this? First, the Spirit will come on you, then the power of the Highest shall overshadow you. Remember the answer or provision is in the power.

And you have all things pertaining to life and godliness by His divine power (Christ), but that power is in the Spirit, so we must wait on the Spirit to Come UP and ON us.

Ephesians 3:16-17 says, *"That he would grant you, according to the riches of his glory, to be strengthened with might by his Spirit in the inner man; That Christ may dwell in your hearts by faith."* The Spirit strengthens you with might (POWER) in the INNER MAN, so that Christ (POWER) may dwell in your hearts (inner man) by faith.

Ephesians 3:20, as well, says, *"Now unto him that is able to do exceeding abundantly above all that we ask or think, according to the power that worketh in us."* If the power is not at work in you, then God cannot do for you exceeding abundantly above what you ask or think (meditate).

Luke11:5-13 says, *"And he said unto them, Which of you shall have a friend, and shall go unto him at midnight, and say unto him, Friend, lend me three loaves; For a friend of mine in his journey is come to me, and I have nothing to set before him? And he from within shall answer and say, Trouble me not: the door is now shut, and my children are with me in bed; I cannot rise and give thee. I say unto you, though he will not rise and give him, because he is his friend, yet because of his importunity he will rise and give him as many as he needeth. And I say unto you, Ask, and it shall be given you; seek, and ye shall find; knock, and it shall be opened unto you. For every one that asketh receiveth; and he that seeketh findeth; and to him that knocketh it shall be opened. If a son shall ask bread of any of you that is a father, will he give him a stone? Or if he asks a fish, will he for a fish give him a serpent? Or if he shall ask an egg, will he offer him a scorpion? If ye then, being evil, know how to give good gifts unto your children: how much more shall your heavenly Father give the Holy Spirit to them that ask him?"*

Here, Jesus teaches on prayer, but also on how to receive the answer in verse 13 where He says, even though you ask for BREAD, the Father GIVES YOU the Spirit, because the provision to your need is in the POWER of the Spirit. Even though the whole prayer from verse 5 to 12 is about asking for bread, yet He ends it off brilliantly with verse 13 by saying, now that you've asked for bread, the Father answers by giving to you the Holy Spirit.

In Acts 4:29-31, it says, *"And now, Lord, behold their threatenings: and grant unto thy servants, that with all boldness they may speak thy word, By stretching forth thine hand to heal; and that signs and wonders may be done by the name of thy holy child Jesus. And when they had prayed, the place was shaken where they were assembled together; and they were all filled with the Holy Ghost, and they spake the word of God with boldness."* Here, we see again the disciples asked for boldness to speak the Word and for miracles, signs, and wonders to be done in the name of Jesus. What do we see? How was their prayer answered? God poured upon them the Spirit, as seen in verse 31.

Most of us, in prayer, when we're asking for a need and the Spirit comes UP and ON US, we shrug Him off. We don't allow Him to finish the operation of taking the provision from inside us and bringing it to us so we can name it or say it just like Jesus Himself said in Mark 11: 24 — *"Therefore I say unto you, What things soever ye desire, when ye pray, believe that ye receive them, and ye shall have them."* When must we believe that we receive? While we pray! There is only one way a person can have strong BELIEF, and that is by the Holy Spirit. 2 Corinthians 4:13 says, *"We having the same spirit of faith, according as it is written, I believed, and therefore have I spoken; we also believe, and therefore speak."* Believing springs from the Spirit of God.

HOW TO
MINISTER THE SPIRIT FOR THE MIRACULOUS

We cannot minister the Spirit to others unless we exercise ministering the Spirit to ourselves first. The moment you sense the presence of the Spirit on your flesh, and you say the GLORY or THE TANGIBLE PRESENCE OF GOD IS HERE, then He manifests Himself to others. 1 Corinthians 12:7 says, "*But the manifestation of the Spirit is given to every man to profit withal.*" Understand that when the power is tangibly felt, it's not so we can have a feeling. Rather, it's for a reason, and that reason is so you can receive your miracle. The anointing is not limited to dancing, praising, singing, or shouting. That is great anyway, but the anointing is not limited to these activities. When the anointing is sensed, we are supposed to find the deaf, the blind, the dumb, the lame, and the demon-possessed to release that anointing on them so they can receive their miracle.

When someone dances under the anointing, we are supposed to profit by that anointing on another, because when they dance like that under the anointing, you can feel the liberty in a place. But, most people don't know what true liberty is, so they resist it or quench it. You can actually step into it when tongues are coming up from your innermost being, and if you keep stirring it up, that gift in you will come UP and ON you and your body will feel it; this is the place you must constantly find yourself in, because it is the place of dominion. We must learn how to co-operate with the anointing when it's present; if we don't, we can miss it.

Let us take an example from the Apostle Peter on how he allowed someone to profit by the anointing he *imparted* to him. Acts 3:1-7 says, "*Now Peter and John went up together into the temple at the hour of prayer, being the ninth hour. And a certain man lame from his mother's womb was carried, whom they laid daily at the gate of the temple which is called Beautiful, to ask alms of them that entered into the temple; who seeing Peter and John about to go into the temple asked alms. And Peter, fastening his eyes upon him with John, said, look on us. And he gave heed unto them, expecting to receive something of them. Then Peter said, Silver and gold have I none; but such as I have give I thee: In the name of Jesus Christ of Nazareth rise up and walk. And he took him by the right hand, and lifted him up:*

and immediately his feet and ankle bones received strength."

You will notice that Peter said to the man "Look on us." What he was saying is, 'Don't be distracted by what's going on around you or by your circumstance. Just look at me because what I am about to give you will not come from a geographical place; neither from above nor from below. It's going to come from inside up and on *me*, then it will flow to you and I don't want you to be distracted from receiving what I am about to give you.' Also, notice that Peter said, *silver and gold have "I" none, but such as "I" have give "I" unto "YOU."* He did not say, 'I will pray so that God may give it so you may receive, but what "I" have, "I" give unto you.' God gave us something to GIVE to the world and that is the SPIRIT or ANOINTING.

I have a favourite scripture to help Christians see we should not wait on God to do what God is waiting on us to do. Let us look closely at what it says in the King James Version of the Bible. Galatians 3:5 says, *"He therefore that ministereth to you the Spirit, and worketh miracles among you, doeth he it by the works of the law, or by the hearing of faith?"* Here, Paul tells us how miracles are ministered to people. I have seen this work not only in my life but also in the life of the saints that come out of the "School of the Spirit," a school of discipleship for Christians, where we teach them HOW TO FLOW IN THE MIRACULOUS.

First, we see the Spirit is ministered, then we see the miracle worked. That means we cannot work miracles without ministering the Spirit first to a person exactly as Peter did in Acts 3:1-8. It can never be by works, because the scripture says in Zechariah 4:6, *"Then he answered and spake unto me, saying, This is the word of the Lord unto Zerubbabel, saying, Not by might, nor by power, but* by my spirit, *saith the Lord of hosts"* (emphasis mine).

THE SPIRIT IS MINISTERED UNTO US BY THE HEARING OF FAITH. I want to show you how this works. When we speak the words of God, then the Spirit who dwells in His words, come on those that hear the spoken words of God. Acts 10:44 reveals, *"While Peter yet spake these words, the Holy Ghost fell on all them which heard the word."* On whom did the Holy Ghost fall? On all who heard the Word!

Then we have another way of ministering the Spirit. Remember I said we cannot minister the Spirit to others unless we minister the Spirit to ourselves. Now look at this scripture, 2 Corinthians 4:13, *"We having the same spirit of faith, according as it is written, I believed, and therefore have I spoken; we also believe, and therefore speak."* When you know that you have the Spirit or let me put it across like this, when you know that you have the Spirit or let me put it across like this, when you are aware of the Spirit and the tangibility of His presence, or when you are conscious of His presence, that is the time to SPEAK or SAY that the Spirit is at hand.

In a meeting I once conducted for believers, I was teaching the word of God on how the miraculous is ministered, when all of a sudden, a young man interrupted the meeting and said, "My wrist was broken in a squash game, can God heal it." I stopped teaching, and said to the people, 'If what I am teaching is from God, then surely God will perform the miracle, not because of what I say, but because He will work with us to confirm His Word with signs following.' Mark 16:20 states, "*And they went forth, and preached everywhere, the Lord working with them, and confirming the word with signs following. Amen.*" I said to the young man, "Come here so that the audience can see." As he came to the altar, I could see he had a brace on his wrist to keep it from getting hurt. I showed the people the wrist and I could see the look on their faces, that look of "IMPOSSIBLE" written all over them.

In the meanwhile, I said, "To prove to you that there are no superstars in the Kingdom of God, I will minister the Spirit to this young man." And I ministered the

Spirit BY SAYING TO HIM, "Now, the moment I lay my hand on your shoulder, you will feel something moving from my hand into your shoulder, and that which you feel will move from your shoulder down into your wrist, and when that happens only then move your wrist from side to side." What was I doing? I was ministering the Spirit to the young man, by what I said, and this is what happened after I asked him, "What do you feel happening in your shoulder?" He said in front of the audience, "I feel something warm moving up and down from my shoulder into my wrist, to my fingertips." The moment he said that I told him, "Move your wrist," and as he moved it, he started to cry and said, "My wrist is healed," and the audience went wild. Many miracles happened that night, but the best thing that happened was when someone came from the audience, and said, "Now I can see it is simple to flow in the miraculous. Thanks, pastor, you've made it easy for us," and I thought to myself, how many people don't know this, but want to do this?

I want to say, the moment you sense the Spirit or Anointing on YOU, that is your cue to do what you could not do, and you'll see the power operating on your behalf because FAITH IS THE CORRESPONDING ACTION TO WHAT YOU BELIEVE IN YOUR HEART.

WHY AND HOW TO PRAY IN TONGUES

The practice of praying in tongues is not so you can show you belong to an elite group, but so you can have direct access to God the Father with no hindrances. One reason the Christian strives to get through to God, is that they think, and are taught that God is in some geographical heavens. Well, in that case, their first priority would be to fight off demonic activity that blocks them from getting through to God. They come up with all kinds of man-made doctrines that make access to God impossible unless they fight the devil first to get through to God. What they are doing is satisfying their own ignorance and their flesh. Jesus already fought the battle and won more than two thousand years ago. Now the Word says that His blood has cleansed the heavens. Hebrews 9:22-23 states, *"And almost all things are by the law purged with blood; and without shedding of blood is no remission. It was therefore necessary that the patterns of things in the heavens should be purified with these; but the heavenly things themselves with better sacrifices than these."*

You now no longer enter the third heaven via the second heaven, of which you were taught that demon spirits or evil angelic beings await you to hold back the answers that God gives. Such preachers use certain scriptures to back up what they say and create a whole lot of false doctrines. We now understand that under the Old Covenant, people were not spiritual but carnal, and the realm connected to the carnal was the second heaven. The temple, under the Old Covenant, was a perfect shape of the human body and a perfect connection to the three heavens. The first heaven connected to the flesh (body) which is the outer court where the entrance was by a gate called *the way*. The second heaven connected to the carnal mind which is the inner court that had an entrance gate called *the truth*. And the third heaven connected to the spirit or heart (innermost being) of a man, which is the HOLY OF HOLIES; and the entrance there is by way of a gate called *the life*.

When Jesus came, He took it—the temple—out of the way and made it redundant, obsolete, and out of use. Hebrews 9:8-10 says *"By this the Holy Spirit points out that the way into the [true Holy of] Holies is not yet thrown open as long as the former [the outer portion of the] tabernacle remains a recognized institution and is still standing, Seeing that that first [outer portion of the] tabernacle was a parable (a visible symbol or type or picture of the present age). In it gifts and sacrifices are offered, and yet are incapable of perfecting the conscience or of cleansing and renewing the inner man of the worshiper. For [the ceremonies] deal only with clean and unclean meats and drinks and different washings, [mere] external rules and regulations for the body imposed to tide the worshipers over until the time of setting things straight [of reformation, of the complete new order when Christ, the Messiah, shall establish the reality of what these things foreshadow—a better covenant]."*

Here, we see that if the former tabernacle is still recognized by anyone, then they cannot enter into the true, which is the innermost of the heart, where Christ is. Hebrews 10:19-20 says, *"Having therefore, brethren, boldness to enter into the holiest by the blood of Jesus, By a new and living way, which he hath consecrated for us, through the veil, that is to say, his flesh."* Now that we have this in order, you can understand that your access to the living God is direct with no hindrance, because the scripture says in 1 Corinthians 14:2, *"For he that speaketh in an unknown tongue speaketh not unto men, but unto God: for no man understandeth him; howbeit in the spirit he speaketh mysteries."* Who is the one who speaks in a tongue speaking to? It says to God. What is he speaking? Mysteries. Now let me explain the mysteries, in 1 Corinthians 4:1, *"Let a man so account of us, as of the ministers of Christ, and stewards of the mysteries of God."* The word of God calls us stewards of the mysteries of God. What does that mean? It means that God, from the beginning when you accepted Christ, has given every answer to you, which is hidden in Christ in you; like for instance, there is a mystery of salvation, a mystery of deliverance, a mystery of healing, a mystery of prosperity and so much more. We are the stewards of those mysteries, and if we do not speak these mysteries out, then the Holy Spirit can have nothing to work within the natural.

In 1 Corinthians 2:7, Scripture says, *"But we speak the wisdom of God in a mystery, even the hidden wisdom, which God ordained before the world unto our glory."* God's wisdom is the treasures of heaven, which is in Christ in us. The provision ordained for us before the foundation of the world, hides in us, which remains a mystery in us in Christ. Only the Spirit of God can help us get into the depth of these mysteries, and one way He does that is when we speak in tongues.

To that effect, Romans 8:26-27 states, *"Likewise the Spirit also helpeth our infirmities: for we know not what we should pray for as we ought: but the Spirit itself maketh intercession for us with groanings which cannot be uttered. And he that searcheth the hearts knoweth what is the mind of the Spirit, because he maketh intercession for the saints according to the will of God.*" What is the will of God for my life? Not even I know this, and this is the weakness every man has, because if we knew, then we would have prayed His perfect will for our lives, apart from the Spirit, in every circumstance we find ourselves in. If it was not hidden from Satan, then he would have known God's plans for us and would have thwarted it at every turn, but it is a mystery not only to us but also to the enemy. The will of God is His redemptive plan for us, which hides in Christ in us and we are the stewards of those mysteries hidden in us.

So, do not be fearful or afraid or nervous to speak in tongues before even the unbeliever, because by praying in a tongue, you are praying the answer according to the perfect will of God in His redemptive plan for you and that unbeliever.

Now, let's get down to how we should pray in tongues. Remember God cannot respond to your tongue if you pray with the idea that God is somewhere out there, but if you pray in a tongue directing it inward, then God will respond with a tongue coming up and outward by His ability. GOD is LOVE. If we do not pray in a tongue, in or out of LOVE towards He who is love, then the tongue is empty. 1 Corinthians 13:1 says, "*Though I speak with the tongues of men and of angels, and have not charity, I am become as sounding brass, or a tinkling cymbal.*" Love will only respond to love. Let's say a person is sick and they need prayer, then you know that you are a steward of the mysteries of healing; because you do not know what is needed at that moment, whether it is a healing or a miracle, neither do you know where the root of the sickness is, only the Spirit knows. So, you need Him to reveal that to you. 1 Corinthians 2:10-11 says, "*But God hath revealed them unto us by his Spirit: for the Spirit searcheth all things, yea, the deep things of God. For what man knoweth the things of a man, save the spirit of man which is in him? Even so the things of God knoweth no man, but the Spirit of God.*" Neither your spirit nor your mind knows the problem, or the answer to the problem because the answer lies in the deep things of God in His redemptive plan. Since the Father, the Son and the Holy Spirit have given us counsel about who we are in Him and spoken every mystery (provision) that will put us over in this redemptive life, then this is the Wisdom of God for us, so that we can walk victorious and glorify Jesus in what we say and do. However, we need the Holy Spirit to search out the deep things of God or Wisdom of God for our life, which is a mystery, but it cannot happen unless we speak that wisdom in a mystery to God, and not to man, because man cannot understand, but God CAN, and the Spirit who knows what to do, will give the answer. So, practice speaking in tongues, because this is the way to the supernatural, primitive Christianity.

www.ingramcontent.com/pod-product-compliance
Lightning Source LLC
Chambersburg PA
CBHW072056040426
42447CB00012BB/3140